Authentic Deconstruction and Composition

Rylah Kluck

BookLeaf Publishing

India | USA | UK

Presentation by *BookLeaf Publishing*

Web: www.bookleafpub.com

E-mail: info@bookleafpub.com

ISBN: 9789363302631

First edition 2024

*To the little girl who always dreamed of being
published one day...*

We did it, this is for you.

ACKNOWLEDGEMENT

Thank you to all the sets of eyes that have read over countless versions of these poems. Thank you to my family, friends, and partner for pushing me, supporting me, and inspiring me in countless ways. Thank you to BookLeaf Publishing for allowing a new poet the opportunity to publish their work!

PREFACE

It all began with bright eyed child,
one who was free and wild.
The world was her oyster,
but she despised sea food,
so what to do?
Find a way to make it work,
put her head down and push through.
These pages tell the story
of how she grew.
Into a woman who uses
a blank page to change her attitude
towards challenges old and new.
Enjoy the happiness and the gloom.

Night Spins

It was a random Saturday in October
& I was nowhere near sober,
had no clue you were coming over.
We had just started getting closure.

It was the yellow American Spirits
& my heart racing, you could hear it.
The surprise in your voice it bit,
but you smiled and lead us back to the pit.

We leapt, my hand in yours,
with light hearts downward we soar.
Until gravity slammed us down, through the
floor
and you were getting out, closing the door.

It's painful how the memory of your touch
& your warm eyes circle around my head so
much.
It whips me around, dizzy and upside down
to the point wrong and right are a jumbled
bunch.

It's more painful that the reality
is you'll always return to her, guiltily.

She has no idea your eyes have met the sea
of mine, after a kiss so raw it momentarily
sets you free.

We have to keep this a secret, he says.
With you it's different, I'm scared.
Until the day he's mine, until I'm truly his,
& I can be with him, not a breath spared.
The day I stop spinning is not near.

Reverse Nirvana

High, up in heaven
Floating with the angels.
Halos written out,
I can't decipher their codes.

Foreign letters and a foreign tongue.
Claiming character flaws that can only be
solved,
the same way they've begun.

Eyes burning from their deceitful fire.
I was too afraid to loosen the grip on my pride,
Accept I had been tricked,
basking in lies.
The magicians cloak vanished to expose...

The fall from heaven, almost too far.
If it weren't for you that saved me,
laid out soft pillows, convincing me
I was ok.
I was solving my problems in the clouds all
night and day.
It was better than the reality of the other side,
they didn't want me to come down and look
around.

Even offered to carry my baggage,
as they played motion pictures of illusions...

A magician's hands, smoke curling from his
fingertips.
Tracing the shape of my lips and distracting me,
while they shoved my baggage underneath.
Into the abyss, where
I watched their halos turn to horns,
how could I accept they had done me wrong?
They're the ones who had kept me safe for so
long.

Overstaying Our Welcome

Your head rests on my pillow,
the train of my thoughts wanders,
my heart the conductor.
Making stops at stations
where you're a part of the future,
but this ticket is round trip.

Last destination is reality,
a place I am not afraid to be,
because I know when you wake up,
You'll roll over, wrap me in your arms, and kiss
me.

Good Morning.
Standing in front of the bathroom mirror,
I've seen this reflection before.
Bags under my eyes,
knowing I could've slept more.

The train horn blasting in my mind
tells me it's time to go.
We've lingered here too long,
missed the next stop,
the route's compromised now.
I wish there was more time

to explore and roam, a person I've never known.
Like clockwork the conductor sounds the horn,
we need to depart now.
We've overstayed our welcome.

Emotional Sickness

Stuck with the in-betweens,
knowing I'd never truly be seen
in a room full of people
and everyone else is living their dream.
While across the scene,
I'm trapped in a nightmare.
A cosmic sorcerer
creating my own being by choosing,
something less than everything.

That's why when I try to swim I sink.
Wearing a scuba suit to the dinner table
and I'm still invisible.
The mask is glued on to conceal the black hole
that has found it's home in the soul of my being.
Engulfing any seed of happiness that dares grow
within me.
Leaves me frozen choosing between
misery and the monster it's creating.

I can let myself sink into that feeling
or act recklessly.
Make decisions that don't represent authenticity.
If I change the habits that consume me, who will
i be?

What will take it's place? Who says I'll be in a
better space?
So I choose to feed the cancerous melancholy,
enabling it's growth by choosing what's
comfortable.
Skeptical of the unknown.

Soaked in disappointment, do I deserve more?
No.
Want to know how I'm sure?
Because I've voluntarily walked away from
every cure.

Dangerous Summits

You can cause more emotional damage then
you're aware of.
By the way your conversation lingers,
trails on,
through the mountains etched in your
subconscious.
Meadows and plateaus of thought.
It's mesmerizing scenery leaving you awestruck.

Roped in and swiftly hooked,
you're the worst kind of drug,
one you never knew you took...

You can't fathom the pain you could and have
already caused.
An avalanche of snow falls,
toppling through and burying any love
that dares climb to the summit.
Only few have reached it's peak.
Every time they're stripped bare and screaming,
'You could hurt me and I wouldn't care!'
But damage isn't what I'd want to cause...
Yet the higher you climb,
the more likely I am to push you off

Farthest Spot in A Parking Lot

When I feel tears prick my eyes
I get in my car and drive,
to a spot in a parking lot
where I can be alone.
'Do not Disturb' on my phone.
Watch the world go by.
It's a place that feels like home,
more than one I've ever known.
Hours will go by, I lose track of time.
29 missed calls, none of which will get a reply.
Leave a voicemail at the tone.
You say you're worried,
but I know there's more to it,
There always is, no matter the circumstance.
Everything isn't as it seems on the surface,
so that's why
I sit in my car and cry.
Watch each soul driving by go about their daily
life...
Wondering who they're going home to,
if they're all alone, or avoiding some unknown.
This must be a developed form of disassociation
because I'm too tired to fight it.
Whatever hurts within me.
So in my car is the best option it seems.

Take Another Look

Wish I could make you do a double take
the way she did.
My beauty neck breaking,
Leaving you a puddle in my wake.
Not sure if it's my own insecurity
or the reality that I know I'm pretty,
just not enough to take your breath away.
Maybe there's more than just beauty
that will make you stay.

Try to cover up my jealousy
cause I know it's a part of me
that's buried deep.
I'm told it's unhealthy,
But all I want is for you to be obsessed with me.
You won't allow yourself it seems
or you just don't subject yourself to that
ideology.

Who am I to you?
It needs to be obvious you want me,
almost seems you don't want her to know the
truth,
only me and you.
So when I see your eyes linger

not once, but twice,
it feels like my heart is on a hook.
You yanked the rod, ripped out a piece, and still
caught me.

Blooming Cement

A flower blooms through cracks in the pavement
between my battered shoes.
Didn't have to ask to,
it just grew.
Brightened up the drab cement,
whispered a suggestion
to change my attitude.
No reason to be so blue
when beauty can grow through the gloom.
The perseverance of it's petals should be enough
proof
that all is needed is a single ray of shining hope
to continue.
Even if it was plucked,
in weeks time it's be replaced with two.
Didn't you know growth is contagious?
It consumes!
Why do you think nature always entombs
dead cities with cobweb filled forgotten rooms?
So, if that's how your heart feels,
beating to the drum of a past tune,
embrace the pain it takes to push through.
The crack in the pavement, it's waiting for you.
The seed is planted,

all you have to do is water the garden of your
soul.
Even if it's cemented over
each drop will take a toll,
eventually erode it and expose the hunger you
have
for new foliage to bloom.
Eager to build a jungle of love just for you.

Full Glass In Hand

It's too good to be true she said
With a volume of voice the windows couldn't
hold in!
Glass shattered.
Cut and battered, she could feel her world
spinning
around her.
Breath ragged with rage,
how could she let herself do this again?
Over and over,
but I Love You.
She said,
to a room full of emptiness,
a heart full of regret,
broken shards her only friend.
He was gone before the words parted her lips...
She could chase him!
Sprint, catch up to the bus stop he was standing
at,
But then it would make the situation public.
And if other ears could hear it,
she would be seen as the bad guy again.
Knowing better than that she grabs a glass,
fills it to the brim with whatever liquor was left,
cheers him in his absence,
and sits silently in her brokenness.

No Hope of Resurrection

How could I detach with such ease?
Why was it easy to ignore me?
Playing hide and seek,
stumbling across my body years later
already decomposing.
Wild animals devoured my heart,
there's nowhere to reattach my emotions
when love tries hitting the restart.

My body may jolt,
but refuse to spark.
Reattachment of an ignition was something a
true mechanic
should be able to do with ease.
But when there's nothing left inside,
there's no hope of being electrified.

A streak of life flashing before your eyes,
I keep going, recognize that I've been telling
myself lies,
another jolt and I turn over…
The want to please, comes from somewhere so
deep,
It's the only way I can resurrect a feeling of
peace.

Disconnect from what I want
To make others happy…

A True Astronautical Expedition

A buzz from the sip of a can,
could send you to the moon my man.
Spring from your heels with rockets forming
smoky tails
that trail on behind you, telling the story
of what the rest of the night will entail.

Wild rides and rapid exhales.
As your fingers grip my waist
my heart rate sails.
Go ahead and take another sip,
maybe then you'll have the courage
to kiss me instead of only admiring my lips.

I've expressed they're in need of companionship.
So climb aboard,
prepare yourself to push the pedal to the floor,
distance yourself from the world and its war.
Finish your drink.
Don't be scared to pour more,
you'll need more fuel to power your touch
to linger.

Discover galaxies with the tips of your fingers.

I need you to take me somewhere that's
undiscovered,
show me it was worth it to join you on this
adventure.

Radical Tectonic Shifts

Forcing my being to shatter,
so while i search for the pieces to put back
together
I can discover slivers I didn't remember
were vital parts of me.

Shards buried beneath the depths of the sea.
They should've been swallowed completely.
Never ceasing to amaze me, my soul has kept
them alive!
The earths core is boiling my deepest insides.
It makes me question of what I'm comprised.

If my soul isn't frozen I may be deserving.
That thought in itself has caused,
the explosion and dissipation of the first edition
I've so humbly titled self love.
Without that natural disaster
I'd still be wallowing, resentment and anger
dictating my decisions and outcomes.
Underneath that heavy blanket of emotion
are abandoned pieces of myself .
They haven't died yet and are eager to help!
Here's to the second edition
of rediscovering myself.

Stagnant Growth

It's crazy how
easy
I can lose pieces of me,
without even realizing
they're missing.
All i feel is the expanse of emptiness growing/
Am i alone in feeling my progress slowing
as I work on it more intentionally?
It could be I'm just hyper focusing,
Or is there a black hole that's engulfing?
If i give in completely,
maybe there's a bottom or an end
shining with relief!
Or I'm trying to twist this perspective positively,
because i can feel myself sinking,
and am scared for the day it completely
encompasses me.
Fear's what's kept me alive so
Why would I not treat it kindly?

Photosynthesis Cures

In solitudic somber.
Meandering around thoughts,
can't help but ponder
what it'd all be like if I'd held onto myself a lil
longer.
Not with an iron grip, but slacked reins.
Claiming on my packaging, "I'm free range"
The cage I've locked myself in
is built from vicious words of self-hatred.

Maybe I need to let go of who I think I am.
Past versions of me multiply.
Monsters I've created inside,
dedicated to sinking their sharp teeth in.
Trauma's bite marks my skin.
I wear long sleeves, concealing the pain within.

So now I must decide,
what pieces of myself do I need to sacrifice?
Let rot and die.
Discover what evolving tastes like.
then maybe I can smile without a caveat.
Bask in the sunrise and let the birds sing.
Somewhere over the hills, far away, outside of
my cage,

I wear a tank top and let the photosynthesis feed
the places within where I've planted new seeds.

An Illusion of a Human

Another night in a row and I'm shocked
you still want to see me.
Illuminated in the dark.
It's hard for me to wrap my head around,
because I can't even stand myself for that long.

My words twisting around a snakes tongue,
forked and contorted.
Taking steps in a direction,
forcing me to sink or swim.
Can't pretend to understand
what lures you in.
Part of me feels as if I'm setting you up for
failure,
painting an illusion of having my shit together.
A concept you've seemed to grasp,
an iron grip on it, you try your hardest,
But if I'm being honest
I don't know why you think I'm eligible for a
job like this...

The description a girl who's your dream vision.
I can try my best and that's all I can promise,
but what if in the end
you regret trying us?

The nights blur together now,
we connected more than I expected
and you struggle to keep your distance.
When you're gone I'll miss this.

Is it too much to ask for,
to find someone who will stay?
Tell me all the ways you perceive me,
what you see that is beautiful underneath.
You act like you have this potential,
to take me as I truly am, illuminate every dark
corner,
but the scariest beasts that live inside are right
before your eyes,
with a smile and a kiss they scream help me.
Lure you in and steal your heart as a prize.

I want you to see me as a this perfect version,
A 2.0 with purpose and direction,
One that doesn't get distracted from her vision.
Can explain to you why she's living, not in her
own bubble
out in the open, lacking indecision.
Leading with direction.

Doomsday Prepper

This pit in my stomach,
it's making me nauseous beyond belief.
How am I to get relief
when I know soon, you're going to leave.
Take with you pieces of me,
that you seemingly cared about, deeply.
I have this feeling
we're about to burst at the seams.
I'll be weak in the knees
and you'll waltz away with the breeze.
Do you think I'm naive?
That I can't see there's more going on behind the
scenes.
This feeling sitting deep within me
is meant to reveal what you've been hiding.
You've guarded yourself, put walls up, built
distrust between us,
and after some quick searching...
Can see your attention isn't on me.
Maybe I don't want to know what you're
thinking.
Maybe you're still lost in the daydream that she's
your one and only.
After seeing all the flaws that embody me,
if you're planning to go at least warn me,

so I can start packing.
Do some sort of preparing.

My Plant Needs a Bigger Pot

You've mellowed out.
Stated as an observation,
Taken as an inclination,
That I'm not the same.
The decisions I've made
Are inducing changes
That are visible outside my own brain.
Shuffling through thoughts
Working to rearrange the wiring of my ways.
The purpose these neural pathways suit is no
longer the same.
It's become easier to cage the insane.
Present confident and charismatic, learning how
to finesse the game,
How much is progress, how much is staged?
What's the definition of growth anyways?
The smile I used to fake that now stays?
The hole in my heart I used to fill with rage,
Is now what I define as decay.
But in a beautiful way!
I don't want to stay the same,
Resurrecting old ways can only end
In tears and pain.
So please don't put yourself through that again…
Come out the other side.

Where the grass is greener,
And your understanding comes from who you
are within,
Not from armor that refused to be reflective.
When this whole self love journey was
beginning,
I never imagined the outside perspective.

Experienced Understanding?

You asked me what I wanted.
A simple answer is expected,
but my mind is calculating at full volume.
All the equations at once.
How are others voices influencing?
What outcome is me
and how is it different from the way I'm
perceived?
It's a more complex question that you think...

If I could, I would want everything,
but I know that's not possible, so I wouldn't call
them dreams.
Aspirations or maybe
just a rest of my eyes as the slumber rolls by.
Visions of the future are too caging.
The what ifs and dramatic dips that this
experience poses
is that of which cannot be predicted.
That's the fun of some of it
the rest leaves me frozen, mortified.
If I can't calculate,
solve for X, find our future,
set the table for two.
What's the point of answering you?

Medusa's Victim

A yearning, a want, a pleading in my heart,
To believe you.
Hold my breath until my face turns blue.
I don't want to know the truth
Or maybe I do.
Discoveries made with subtly laid clues.
Self doubt is a disease I subject myself to,
And there's proof!
It kept me safe before you.
What if the way you look at me turns me to
stone?
Carves me into a delicate statue.
Would you admire me?
Place me on a pedestal in the middle of your
mind,
For all your thoughts to see,
Or do I need to accept that you're not ready
To bask in this level of beauty.
Let me teach you!
Don't take your love from me,
I want to see you completely.

Loving Eyes

There are times when I look at you,
I can see it so clearly.
This scene I've started to paint.
Mixing a palate of primary colors, beautiful in
the most simple ways.

A stroke added to the canvas with every smile,
the way your chocolate eyes make me melt.
Why would i stop my brain from dreaming far
ahead now?
Dipping the brush in with anticipation, my heart
stirring shades,
all the while...
My brain screams I'm running away with my
creativity somehow!
I always have.

I'm yearning to show you how my past colors
have combined
Layered to create the unique hue i call mine.
I hope you can see the beauty in the old,
chipped, and faded.
Maybe not the best foundation anymore,
but without those shades, I'd be a comparable
bore.

So come paint with me darling!
Help me dip my toe into a bright new palatable
soul,
One enriched with color choices of your own.
I want to see where we can go, leave our brushes
on the table
And call each other home

Slow Down and Take A Look Around

Ivy climbs brick by brick by brick
up a building.
Beautifying its stationary and deteriorating
existence.
What a beloved sight it is!
To witness growth support the decay,
hold it in place,
so it's history can remain.
It'll spread through the stone.
Crawl inside and take hold.
Unrelenting and purposefully constructing
a whole new world.
While honoring what allowed it to flourish.
The structure is solid,
will not compromise,
and over time the leaves will turn brown,
wilt on the sides.
Fall to the wet cement below.
Imprint it's dying image, make one last wish.
Until next spring,
when the vines of ivy flourish again.

www.ingramcontent.com/pod-product-compliance
Lightning Source LLC
LaVergne TN
LVHW010829200726
843508LV00012B/2537